1: The Parish Church of St. Mary.
2: The Churchyard lychgate.

PAINSWICK
"Queen of the Cotswolds"

The best known building in Painswick is the Parish Church of St. Mary, which sits so beautifully in one of the most memorable churchyards in the country. Its legendary ninety-nine yew trees are said to be impossible to count - and that the hundredth will never grow. The oldest yews were planted in 1792.

The original Norman church - mentioned in the Domesday Book - has been gradually replaced in later centuries. The present north aisle was built during Richard II's reign (1377-1399), and rebuilt in 1480, along with the central nave and St. Peter's chapel of the lords of the manor.

The tower was also built in 1480, although the lofty steeple was not added until 1637. The south aisle was constructed in 1741 with further alterations completed in 1877. In 1883 the church was struck by lightening, bringing down about one-third of the spire. Portions fell through the roof causing much damage.

The tower houses twelve bells, the earliest of which dates from 1686. They are well known to ringers all over the country, as being unsurpassed in harmony and beauty.

A TOUR AROUND PAINSWICK

Starting opposite the Church at the Town Hall, look ahead to St. Mary's Church and Churchyard, then right towards some of Painswick's imposing Cotswold houses - particularly Beacon House, an 18th century town house, and the Falcon Inn, built in 1711. Look left, down Victoria Street where the buildings become smaller residential cottages.

Walk through the Churchyard noting the yews and fine alter tombs. The marks on the tower and east and west Church walls were made by cannon and musket fire during the Royalist assault on Painswick in 1644. Leaving by the gate leading into the end of St. Mary's Street, turn left to find the stocks which are of great historical interest. They are early 17th century iron 'spectacle' stocks - one of only two examples remaining today. Looking along St. Mary's Street note Loveday's House - until recently the vicarage - a perfect example of a small 18th century Cotswold family home.

Move from the end of St. Mary's Street into Hale Lane which has fine trees and large Cotswold stone houses (on right). The largest of these are Court House - said to be on the site of Painswick's original manor house - and Castle Hale - thought to be on the site of Pain Fitzjohn's now vanished 12th century castle. At the lower end of Hale Lane walk through the narrow passage known as the Churn and turn right into Kemps Lane - some of the large stones in the wall on the right as you walk down, are said to be from Pain Fitzjohn's castle.

Continue down Kemps Lane then Knapp Lane to the bottom where you will see before you the picturesque Painswick Mill.

Returning to the Churn continue up Kemps Lane passing the Painswick Hotel - once the vicarage. Turn left into Tibbiwell Lane - note the fine wrought iron sign of the former Golden Heart Inn to the left.

Arriving at the cross, turn right and walk past the Royal Oak Inn and Loveday's Garden - another fine Cotswold house. Turn right into Vicarage Street, with its many fine stone cottages, go down past Yew Tree House and the classical Dover House and turn right down a little footpath passing the Friends Meeting House - built in 1706. From here the path leads down to Brookhouse Mill.

Walk back to St. Mary's Street via Tibbiwell Lane and turn right then left into Friday Street - said to be the site of the original market. Walk up and turn left into Bisley Street and note the splendid 14th century doorway to The Chur, on the right. As with many of Painswick's houses The National Trust Bookshop was a weaver's cottage in the early 17th century - and before that "The Inn" of Painswick.

Down New Street is the Post Office - a fine half timbered property which dates back to the building of the street in 1428. Return to the end of Bisley Street and walk into Gloucester Street. About half way up turn and look back at the splendid view down Gloucester Street and Bisley Street - which formed the main streets of Painswick in the 13th century - to Longridge Woods in the distance.

At the top of Gloucester Street take the right fork and follow the main road (B4073), until you arrive at the entrance (on the left) to Painswick House and the famous Rococo Garden - which is open to the public and well worth visiting.

If you walk through the beech plantations on the right of the main road, you will come out onto the open common and be rewarded on a clear day with a striking view of the Spoonbed Valley and the long crest of the Cotswold escarpment, to the River Severn in the vale beyond.

Discover more with the maps on page 7.

THE PHOTOGRAPHS

1: Painswick's 17th century stocks.
Their position near the Church and the old Court House is the traditional site of such instruments of correction.
2: Ancient gravestones in the Churchyard.
3: Lamp House in Victoria Square.
4: Loveday's House in St. Mary's Street.
5: 19th century bow windows in St. Mary's Street.
6: The Royal Oak Inn in St. Mary's Street.

7: Beacon House and The Fiery Beacon in New Street adjacent to Victoria Square.
8: Bisley Street, one of the oldest streets in Painswick.
9: The Rococo Garden in early spring.
10: Victoria Street - the Town Hall Entrance, commercial and residential cottages.
11: Painswick House.

HISTORIC LANDSCAPE

Although there is evidence of neolithic, bronze and iron age occupation in the area, Painswick Beacon was the home of the first known inhabitants of Painswick. Here enormous ramparts of an ancient Celtic hill fort surround the highest point in the Parish.

In later centuries some Romano-Britons built a fine villa on the spur at Ifold, where today stands a splendid Cotswold farm house now named Highfold. The clearing of the forest covered valleys for farmland commenced in the Spoonbed area at this time.

During the Saxon period an area around what is now St. Mary's Churchyard was cleared and a small "Wicke" (a Saxon word for Village) was built. The first known Lord of the Manor of Painswick was Ernisi, who lived during the reign of Edward the Confessor.

After the Norman conquest the Manor was rewarded to Walter de Lacy and then from his heirs to Pain Fitzjohn - from whom Painswick takes its name. He built a small castle on the site of what is now Castle Hale. By the 12th century it was the largest manor in the county. The manor expanded its agricultural lands over the centuries and many of the Lords were members of noble families, closely connected with significant historical events.

Painswick played an important part in the Civil War - there were many skirmishes in the area and in 1643 King Charles I spent the night at Court House before the siege of Gloucester.

Painswick's prosperity, her splendid streets and farmhouses, and the beauty of the surrounding countryside - has been largely shaped by the areas association with the wool trade, which rose to its peak between 1750 and 1800. At one time 30 mills turned water into power within the Parish, and many of the fine country houses and farms were built on the wealth of the mill owners and clothiers.

Illustration: The pagan God Pan, does he preside over Painswick?

PAINSWICK
Pictorial Guide

INFORMATION

Painswick Tourist Information - in the Library (open Easter to November). Tel: 01452 813552
Stroud Tourist Information - in the Subscription Rooms, Stroud. Tel: 01453 765768

Places of interest:

The Rococo Garden - open January to November.

Leisure and Recreation:

The Painswick Institute - has regular exhibitions of fine art and quality crafts.

Painswick has a recreation ground and Sports Club - with facilities for rugby, football, tennis and cricket. There are two bowling greens - one reputed to be the oldest and finest in England. An excellent 18-hole golf course can be found on Painswick Beacon.

Painswick Squash Club - at the east end of Wick Street near Bulls Cross. The Blues Room - at the same location - has regular live music.

Eating and drinking:

The Painswick Hotel, in Kemps Lane.
Painswick Inns - The Falcon Inn, opposite the Churchyard in New Street.
The Royal Oak Inn, in St. Mary's Street.
Other Inns in the area - The Butchers Arms in Sheepscombe, The Edgemore Inn at Edge and The Woolpack Inn in Slad.
There are excellent restaurants and a number of good tea/coffee houses in Painswick.

Accommodation:

The Painswick Hotel, The Falcon Inn and many Bed & Breakfast addresses in Painswick and the area - ask the Tourist Information for a list.

Festivals, fairs and shows:

The Clipping of the Church - Sunday following 19th September at St. Mary's Church.
The Painswick Victorian Fair - is held in July.
Painswick Show - is held every August.

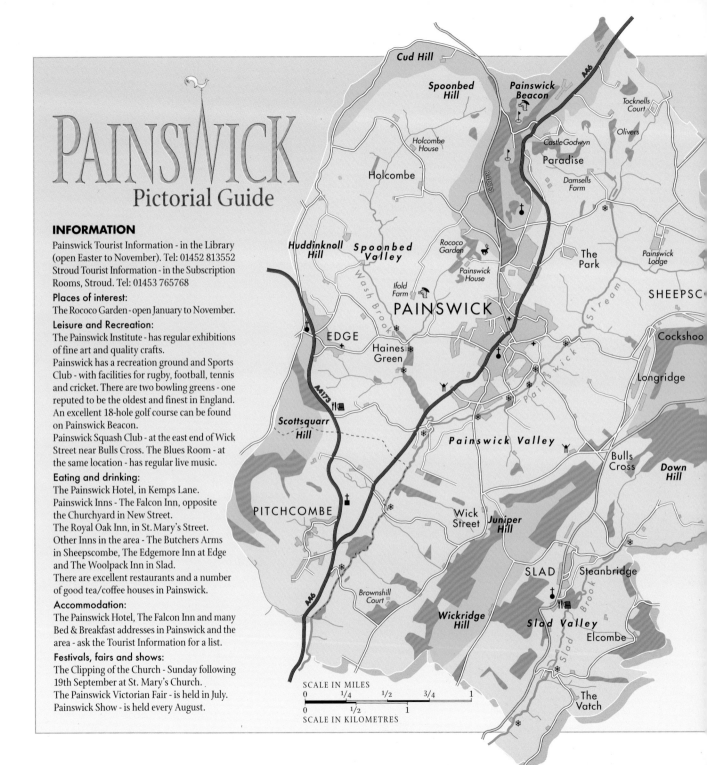

SCALE IN MILES
0   1/4   1/2   3/4   1

0   1/2   1
SCALE IN KILOMETRES

THE PARISH OF PAINSWICK
including the Parish of Pitchcombe

Ebworth

Far End

N W E S

PAINSWICK STREET MAP

To Painswick House and Rococo Garden

GLOUCESTER ROAD
GYDE ROAD
Gyde House
CHELTENHAM ROAD
A 46
Health Centre
CANTON ACRE
BUTT GREEN
PULLENS ROAD
UPPER WASHWELL
Police & Fire St.
LOWER WASHWELL LANE
N W E S
THE CROFT
School
CHURCHILL WAY
GLOUCESTER STREET
Recreation Ground
HYETT CLOSE
HOLLYHOCK LA.
ASHWELL
BISLEY STREET
Institute
VICARAGE STREET
BLACKWELL MEAD
HAMBUTTS DRIVE
HAMBUTTS END
Post Office
NEW STREET
Town Hall
FRIDAY ST.
Friends Meeting Hall
EDGE LANE
VICTORIA ST.
ST. MARYS STREET
The Cross
WC
TIBBIWELL LANE
St. Mary's Church
Library
WC
Hotel
HALE LANE
Court House
KEMPS LANE
A 46
P
Castle Hale
STROUD ROAD
STAMAGES LANE
KNAPP LANE
KINGSMILL LANE
GREENHOUSE LANE
Brookhouse Mill
Capp Mill
Painswick Mill
COTSWOLD MEAD
KINGSMILL LANE

KEY TO AREA MAP
- Buildings
- Woodland
- Hills/Valleys
- ✝ Church/Chapel
- Restaurant
- Inn/Pub
- Country Park
- Golf Course
- Sports Club
- Water Mill
- Site of Antiquity

KEY TO STREET MAP
- Buildings
- 🍴 Restaurant
- ☕ Tea/Coffee House
- 🍴🍺 Inn/Pub
- ✉ Post Office
- ⛽ Garage
- 🅿 Car Park
- Tennis Court
- Bowling Green
- WC Public Convenience
- ℹ Tourist Information

Cartography © 1998 NICHOLAS J. JONES GRAPHICS

7

Sheepscombe

Sheepscombe valley twists away to the east of Painswick, below beautiful beech woods protecting undulating slopes of pasture land. Once a medieval tithing of Painswick Manor, a valley of ancient woodland, a deer park enjoyed by the manorial lords. Painswick Lodge was developed after 1400 - a house which welcomed Henry VIII and Anne Boleyn in 1535 and is reputed (along with Court House in Painswick) to have once been the Manor House of Painswick.

In 1700 the deer park was broken up and in the following century scattered farms appeared as land became tenanted. The village began to grow in size and the plentiful water supply from hillside springs attracted clothiers and clothworkers to the area. Dwellings were altered and newly erected to cater for the cottage industry of weaving. In about 1802 the Wright brothers from Tetbury took over the village mill increasing local employment in the textile trade.

The reputation of the villagers in the 19th century was unenviable, due partly to the abundance of ale houses. In 1819 Charles Neville, curate at Painswick, gathered funds for the building of the church, which was completed within a year by the villagers.

After 1830 the mill began to fail despite being fitted with steam power. Within a decade it had closed. The ensuing loss of work was an economic disaster for the valley and the population was affected, falling from 803 in 1831 to 510 in 1861. Dwellings were left empty and fell into ruin. Those who remained struggled to work the land and only a few craftsmen, tradesmen and labourers survived. The population had fallen to only 383 by 1921.

By the 20th century, people had begun to come to Sheepscombe again - seeking beauty and peace. The village has grown and prospered in its wonderful location.

THE SHEEPSCOMBE PHOTOGRAPHS

1: *Coldstream Cottage and the Village Hall in the centre of the village.*

2: *A Cotswold barn at Lodge Farm near Sheepscombe.*

3: *The Butchers Arms.*

4: *The Church of St. John the Evangelist in Sheepscombe.*

5: *Sheepscombe Valley after a dusting of snow.*

Illustration: An ancient doorway at Painswick Lodge.

Sheepscombe Valley

9

Edge

A mile to the west of Painswick lies the village of Edge. It lies across the Spoonbed Valley straddling a hilltop. For this reason, it probably derives its name from the word 'rudge' or ridge.

Like Edge, Spoonbed was one of the original four tithings of Painswick - and probably the first part of the ancient manor to be cleared of forest. The 3rd century Romano-British villa found at Ifold - in its fine position on a tongue of land - would have seen some of the first organised agriculture in the Painswick area.

The Gloucester convent of Llanthony for four centuries held a considerable amount of land in the valley between Painswick and Edge, while the Abbey of St. Peter in Gloucester farmed Scottssquarr and the land lying to the west of Horsepools, after about 1086.

In the nineteenth century the Spoonbed Valley contained four mills. One has now been demolished and the other three converted into homes - as are all the other mills in the parish.

The approach from Painswick into the main part of the village of Edge runs close by two greens which provide a picturesque setting for the surrounding houses - the larger being a perfect example of a Cotswold village green.

The church at the centre of the village was built in 1866 as a chapel of ease to Painswick and became a parish church for parts of Painswick, Pitchcombe, Harescombe and Haresfield in 1873.

To the west of Edge lies Scottssquarr Common, an area of special scientific interest where many wild flowers and butterflies proliferate. From this spot - and many others in the village there are spectacular views of the Malvern Hills, Brecon Beacons and across the Painswick Valley.

THE EDGE PHOTOGRAPHS
1: The larger of the two village greens in Edge.
2: Ifold (now Highfold) Farm.
3: Edge Hill Farm after January snow.
4: The Church of St. John the Baptist, Edge.
5: The village viewed from The Edgemore Inn.
Illustration: Roman fibula found at Ifold Roman villa.

Edge and the Spoonbed Valley

Slad

Millions of people are familiar with Slad through Laurie Lee's book "Cider with Rosie". His poetic reminiscences of childhood in the Slad Valley create a vivid picture of Cotswold life between the wars. At that time there was a squire in Steanbridge House who owned the Estate, a vicar in the Vicarage, a school teacher in the School House and the school full of children. There were several farms in the valley and workers living in the cottages.

By the time his book had been adapted for television in the early 1970s, the millions who saw it were looking at a thing of the past. While the valley remained a place of great natural beauty, social change had been very rapid.

The Museum in Gloucester has votive tablets from a Roman villa found in the Slad Valley. One has a carving of Romulus with a double horn of plenty resting on a tiny altar. In this guise he was a fertility god, there to protect crops. The earth and its fruits were the chief concern then and they stayed that way for hundreds of years. According to Volume Eleven of the Victoria History of Gloucester "...the village of Slad originated at Steanbridge, an important crossing of the Slad Brook, recorded in 1353, which carried the Painswick-Cirencester road near the site of a Roman villa."

Civil War apart, the land was still the chief preoccupation on the 9th August 1643 when King Charles 1 led his troops over the brook at Steanbridge. He was on his way to Gloucester - held by the Parliamentarian Colonel Massey - and came up over Bulls Cross to spend the night at Painswick.

Processing the fruits of the soil was recorded in the Slad Valley as early as the 13th century. Grain and woollen mills were recorded through the reigns of Henry VIII and Queen Elizabeth I up to the late 19th century when there was a dozen mills in the Slad Valley.